THE FIRST YEAR

First Printing, 2017

The first year molds our attitude towards school.

Thanks to you, ours is
POSITIVE,
AWESOME,
SUPER COOL!

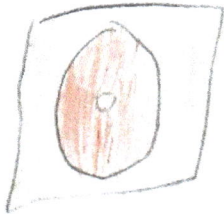

Each morning you greet us with
a smile ear-to-ear.

No wonder it's been such a
WONDERFUL year.

We've learned to
READ,
WRITE,
WALK IN A LINE…
SOLVE PROBLEMS,
TIE SHOES,
AND SHARE WHAT'S MINE.

You say silly things
we repeat back in turn.

Your gift is making it so
FUN TO LEARN.

We LOVE RECESS and
know you do too,
the SILLIES SHAKE OUT
and we come back renewed.

When we throw a tired and
frustrated fit,
you stick by our side and
DON'T LET US QUIT.

We've become independent over this year.
For that we are PROUD and our parents CHEER!

You treat us as if we are
one of your own.
We are OH SO GRATEFUL
for the love you have shown.

Soon the classroom noise
will be no more, no
GIGGLES
or
PITTER-PATTER
of feet on the floor.

WELCOME
TO
Kindergarten
1 2 3

When the artwork comes down
and the halls are all bare,
please DON'T FORGET
how much we all care.

Our FIRST YEAR of school
has come to an end,
a big THANKS to you,
our TEACHER and FRIEND.

www.ingramcontent.com/pod-product-compliance
Lightning Source LLC
Chambersburg PA
CBHW040304100426
42811CB00011B/1357